CODING CHAMPIONS

TIMOTHY AMADI

Torchflame Books

Durham, NC

Copyright © 2019 Timothy Amadi
Coding Champions
Timothy Amadi
www.bugzero.codes
timothy@bugzero.codes

Published 2019 by Torchflame Books
www.torchflamebooks.com
Durham, NC 27713 USA
SAN: 920-9298

ISBN: 978-1-61153-350-7

About bugzero.codes

Hi, we are Timothy, Eugene and Daniel.
No matter what you do or how old you are,
everyone can code.
Follow us on our coding adventure at:

www.bugzero.codes

BUGZERO.CODES

BRINGING KIDS TO TECH

$a = 0.75 - 0.25 * float$

TO ASSIST PEOPLE WHO ARE SICK, MEDICAL TECHNOLOGY HELPS PEOPLE GET BETTER QUICK!
AND TO VIEW OUTER SPACE LIKE COOL PICTURES OF MARS, SPACE PROGRAMS HELP PEOPLE SEE PLANETS AND STARS!
HAVE YOU EVER WONDERED HOW CARTOONS HAVE A CERTAIN LOOK AND FEEL? MODELING TECHNOLOGY MAKES ANIMATED CHARACTERS LOOK REAL!

MORE BUGZERO.CODES BOOKS

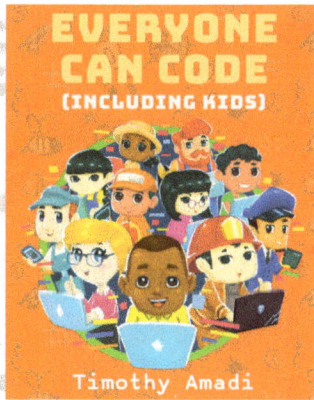

Everyone Can Code - Including Kids
With rhyming text and colorful illustrations, this fun book encourages children of all ages to explore the wonderful world of coding. With code that helps a plumber identify a clogged sink, alerts a firefighter to a new fire, tells a chef when her food is ready and identifies pests on a farmer's crop, children will learn practical ways they can make the world a better place through coding.

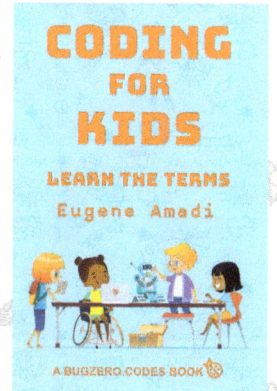

Coding for Kids: Learn the Terms
Written by a kid for kids, this book offers a brief overview of more than 25 basic terms essential for coding. Fun puzzles and activities keep the lessons accessible and help kids learn the terms so they can start coding on their own.

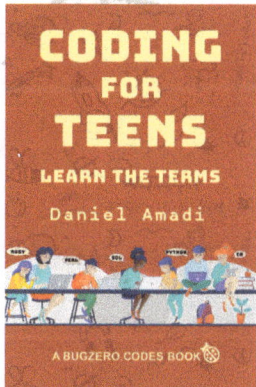

Coding for Teens: Learn the Terms
Teens are discovering the fun and usefulness of coding, from gaming to social media to creating apps to building their college resume. But it can be daunting to get started. There are so many programming languages and new words to learn.
This book, written by a teen author is a great introduction to coding terms.

Cybersecurity for Teens: Learn the Terms
Teens have access to millions of apps and hundreds of connected products, including computers, smartphones, and even smart sneakers. These digital tools are fun and useful for everything from from gaming to social media, to homework, to online purchases. But the digital world can be dangerous unless one knows the risks and how to avoid them.

Coding is Fun
For the naturally curious, this coloring book is a fun and educational introduction to the many ways that coding affects our daily lives. From remote control cars to video calls to laundry machines to drip irrigation, coding makes the modern world work. An introduction to the wonders of coding with 30 original illustrations in a coloring book that will feed curiosity.

**Follow Timothy, Eugene and Daniel
on their coding adventures at:
www.bugzero.codes**

BUGZERO.CODES

BRINGING KIDS TO TECH